VOYAGEURS

NATIONAL PARK

by
GREG BREINING

with photography by
J. ARNOLD BOLZ

LAKE STATES INTERPRETIVE ASSOCIATION
INTERNATIONAL FALLS, MINNESOTA

LAND OF ROCK, FOREST AND WATER

We skip along the waves of Namakan Lake in a large motorboat as a stone skims a pond. If we stand clear of the windshield, the wind blows strong against our faces, pulling against our skin and hair. Two hundred years ago the French-Canadian voyageurs could not have imagined such speed. We pass pelicans, loons, cormorants, mergansers and gulls. The water and forest and rock are a kaleidoscope, the islands slipping behind shore and the shore behind islands, the cold cliffs numb to the glitter of sun from the waves.

It is a view of Voyageurs National Park that is familiar to many who boat the big waters of Rainy, Namakan, Kabetogama or Sand Point lakes. And it is not a bad place to begin. But there is far more than this—things many people never see: the scrub-oak barrens on the open ridges on the Cruiser Lake Trail; the long vistas from the outcrops overlooking Lost Bay on Kabetogama Lake, or the cliffs near Lucille Lake; the star-filled sky above an island campsite in Namakan Narrows; the chain of small lakes in the interior of the Kabetogama Peninsula, which lie within a geologic fault much like a river gorge; a beaver pond along one of the foot trails on the peninsula; the beauty of dark green conifers against clean white snow.

The region was called by one early traveler, long deprived of civilized comforts, a "desert of rock, forest, and water." It is a varied country where the interplay of those elements is continual. The park itself is 219,000 acres. At its center is the Kabetogama Peninsula. One-third of the park is water, most of it contained in four large lakes: Kabetogama, Namakan, Sand Point, and the giant Rainy, where wind can build in a clear fetch that in places exceeds 35 miles. Hundreds of small islands dot the lakes. More than two dozen small lakes (and many smaller ponds and bogs) mark the land in the park. It is a park based on water, and in fact is most easily seen in summertime from a boat.

Voyageurs can be appreciated by its contrasts, the ironies of the area.

The land is very old. Much of the bedrock was formed 2.7 billion years ago, long before the appearance of such familiar landforms as the Rockies or Appalachians or the Grand Canyon. Yet the land is also very young, its appearance owing to the devastating effects of glaciers only 11,000 years ago.

The wild beauty of Voyageurs National Park is apparent—upclose in lichens and ferns, and (opposite) in this broad overview of Anderson Bay, Rainy Lake.

The southern boreal forest . . . the "north woods."

The land is flat yet very rugged. The lowest point in the park is the surface of Rainy Lake at an average of 1,107 feet above sea level; the highest ground are the hills three miles south of Namakan Lake, the tallest reaching less than 300 feet above the water. Yet within this limited range of topography are innumerable sheer cliffs and steep hills and outcrops. The evidence of this ruggedness is the sweat on a hiker's brow and the heaviness in his legs.

Voyageurs is a land of harsh contrasts in weather. A hot July day can exceed 90 degrees. Yet on a star-filled January night the cold sets down hard, occasionally reaching minus 35, a temperature that immediately takes your breath. In such cold, one fervently appreciates summer, as short as it is. The last killing frost may visit in late May; the first, in early September—a growing season of scarcely more than 100 days. Despite the abundance of water, precipitation is only moderate—about 24 inches a year, a fifth of which is snow.

Voyageurs is natural land preserved. Established in 1975, it is unique among this country's national parks as an example of the southern boreal forest—what is sometimes called simply the "north woods." It is a mix of black spruce, balsam fir and northern white cedar, stands of giant red pine and white pine and an amalgam of hardwoods such as aspen, paper birch and oak. Its inhabitants include moose, wolves, black bears, ravens, white-tailed deer, beaver, bobcats, lynx, white pelicans, loons, bald eagles, ospreys, great blue herons and many more.

Yet Voyageurs is also a land rich in human history and affected in many ways by human use. The park's waterways were a key stretch of a centuries-old "voyageurs' highway" from the Great Lakes west and northward into the interior of the western United States and Canada. Voyageurs was named for these French-Canadian canoemen who 200 years ago transported trade goods and furs on the big lakes along the international border, including Sand Point, Namakan and Rainy. Even earlier, this water route along the northern border was used by the first European explorers seeking the fabled and elusive Northwest Passage to the Pacific and for hundreds or thousands of years before that by the Indians who settled this country and invented the ingenious and indispensable birch-bark canoe.

From the air it is possible to recognize immediately the value of the canoe to early travelers or the worth of a boat to modern-day visitors. Lakes, ponds and streams stretch out in all directions. This is a water-based park, true to its name. As the Indians and voyageurs of old knew, it often is insane to climb outcrops, wade through beaver ponds, sink to your thighs in peat bogs, and fight brush when a canoe or boat will carry you to the far corners. So in visiting the park, remember that, and see it first from water level, where rock and forest and lakes touch. But then, when you have seen it from that perspective, push inland, walk a trail, sit by a beaver pond, stand on a bald rock outcrop high above the lakes and experience the things few others take the time to see.

Rock and forest and lakes touch at water level inviting adventure in boat or canoe.

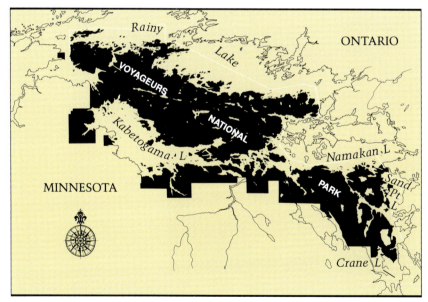

VIEWS OF THE PARK

The Wolf Pack Islands—of which there are three—lie near the international border in the midst of Namakan Lake. To reach them from either Crane Lake to the south or Ash River or Kabetogama to the west requires a slalom through islands and channels. We were dropped off on the westernmost island one day in July. We immediately set out to explore—not an ambitious task since our island was no more than a couple hundred yards long.

Wolf Pack West is not greatly different from dozens of other small islands in Voyageurs. It and its sisters are spits of bedrock—glacial left-behinds—that were slowly colonized by plants, whose seeds and spores blew over or were carried by birds from the mainland. Over thousands of years the life and death of plants and small animals built a pitifully thin soil. A gardener marooned here would weep at the sight of it. Our particular island was covered by large red pines. Reaching about 70 feet high and a couple feet across, most seemed all of the same age. This stand of pine probably sprang from a forest fire that swept the island a century ago or more, judging by the size of the trees. Since then, they have become the dominant trees on this patch of rock, blocking the sunlight from competing trees and in the process casting their spell over our island. It was something of a magic forest beneath the pines, where only low-lying shrubs and runty trees grew. Our footsteps were cushioned by needles as we moved among the blueberry bushes, gathering ripe fruit.

Our island had a sandy beach and campsite, where we set our tents. We swam briefly but then sat back to survey the nearly calm lake around us. A few herring gulls flew by. Occasionally we saw a loon swimming in the distance. Had we taken in this view 200 years ago, we may have seen voyageurs in the distance, paddling their 25-foot birch-bark canoes. Eight men to a canoe, they would have pulled quickly at their paddles—a beat a second—as they sang French songs of drinking, working, sport and romance. They might have stopped for a "pipe," a rest while they smoked for several minutes, before picking up their paddles and resuming their course down the lake toward the portage at Kettle Falls. We ourselves might have been Ojibways encamped at this very spot because of its easy, sandy landing and favorable exposure.

Afternoon turned quickly to twilight, a brief, brilliant sunset marking the transition. Stars appeared in the deepening indigo sky.

More than 900 islands, many richly forested, dot the lakes in the park.

As we finished our dinner, the mosquitoes started theirs, and we retired to the tents until the sun illuminated our island once again.

We parked the car on the ice road at the west end of the Kabetogama Peninsula and set out under leaden skies, the wind skating raw off Rainy. The ski trail began in the crackling, brittle marsh grass and wound through uplands, past dark green balsam fir and outcrops bigger and grayer than elephants. The trail itself was superb, tracked and easy to ski, but our sled was obstinate. On the turns it attempted to escape, sailing off into the woods behind me and nearly jerking me over backwards. It defeated my best efforts to ski uphill. I unsnapped my skis, tucked them under my arm and walked. I talked to myself—loudly, to be heard over the sound of my pounding heart and head. How in the name of all that is good on this earth did the Indians and voyageurs and trappers travel this country in winter?

We rounded a bend in the trail, where a large white pine sprouted from a bluff. We looked out over a broad lowland and beaver pond. The beaver lodges made white humps, like igloos, under the snow. There the beaver wintered, secure from wolves, moving by underwater passageways beneath the ice, living off aspen saplings and branches cached at the pond bottom. The beaver, besides having grasping hands and long buck teeth to down and limb trees, has other adaptations that help in this task. Valves in the nose and ears shut as the animal submerges, and transparent membranes shield its eyes as goggles would. Its lips close behind its teeth so that it can carry branches in its mouth without drowning. Its thick woolly underfur allows it to swim and work though the water may be barely warmer than freezing. The beaver seems well adapted to its specific niche—better adapted than I to the niche in which I now found myself. As the wind whipped a dusting of snow across the open marsh, I pulled my wool hat down to cover my neck.

The trail turned back into the woods, beneath the spreading shelter of the red and white pine that populated a ridge. We traded off with the sled, but my friends found the going as tough as I did. We decided to set up a base camp, where we could leave our gear. We left the trail and the ridge, wading through the snow into a suitable hollow protected by spruce and balsam fir. We shoveled and tramped out a site in the snow and erected a lightweight tent.

To travel in this raw and breathtaking season is to wonder at the perseverance of the Indians, voyageurs and trappers.

Broad, glistening winter landscapes beckon to hardy outdoorspeople.

Our camp set, we strapped on our skis again and set out on the trail once more, this time leaving the contemptible sled to fend for itself.

Freedom! The forest sailed by. We flew down the trails—through the pines, birch and aspen thickets on the uplands, down the hills into the black spruce, ash groves and white-cedar swamps in the lowlands. The wind generated in our downhill flight stung our cheeks and noses. We stopped to observe what wildlife we could. An occasional raven flapped black against the lead sky—the ubiquitous raven, with us in the north woods as though it were woof in the fabric of the sky. A bundle of sticks—some of them near-logs—sat in the top of a tall, dead tree at the margin of a beaver pond. It was the nest of an osprey, or "fish hawk." Occasionally along the ski trail we found pellets of moose and deer and the hair-filled scat of wolves or coyotes. We saw a depression where a ruffed grouse had burrowed for the night.

As darkness settled in, we returned to our camp. We fixed and ate dinner, ignoring the begging of a Canada jay, or "whiskey jack." When shadows became night, we settled into our positions around the campfire, waiting long hours for sleepiness to catch up with us.

A heavy iron ring six inches across is anchored in a large outcrop at the south end of the Cruiser Lake Trail. A relic of logging days, it was used as an anchor point in manipulating acres of logs that floated in Lost Bay. This bay, on Kabetogama Lake, has sloping, wooded shores (in contrast to the precipitous cliffs along much of Rainy). Two beaver lodges occupied the particular cove where I stood. At water's edge are emergent aquatic plants—cover for ducks, wading birds and other animal life. Out from the shoreline are shallows covered with not only ledgerock, but also a whole range of boulders, gravel, sand and muck. If you fish for smallmouth bass, this sort of thing stirs great excitement, because it provides cover for an abundance of crayfish, nymphs of dragonflies and mayflies, caddis fly larvae, and other invertebrates on which the bass feed. The chain of life does not stop there. All sorts of animals are dependent on these shallow bays, among them the kingfisher that sat in the gray, dead snag down the shore from me and the great blue heron wading the cattails for frogs.

My destination was Rainy Lake, which lay at the other end of the trail, 10 miles away. I was to be picked up there in six hours.

Built of interwoven branches and sticks of aspen, willow, birch and other lowland trees, beaver dams are incredibly tough.

Ten miles in six hours is mighty slow walking. In fact I saw myself getting there in four and then submitting to mosquitoes for two. So I began with a couple of loops at the beginning of the trail and generally occupied myself with the things around me.

The trail climbed quickly from the lake and then dropped just as fast. Almost immediately I came upon a section of woods that was flooded—and with it the trail. I hopped stump to log for awhile, waded a bit, and then came across the cause of this. A beaver had built a stick and earthen dam just downstream of the trail on a tiny creek, backing water up across the trail and a couple of acres of woods as well. Beaver dams are incredibly tough, built of interwoven branches and sticks of aspen, willow, birch and other lowland trees. The aspen sticks, in particular, are peeled of their bark, which the beavers have eaten. Many dams are packed with mud, as this one was, to further seal and stabilize the mass. Left intact, the dam would flood out what was now live timber, creating a margin of standing deadwood around the beaver pond. By extending the boundaries of its pond, the beaver was creating access to new areas of the forest—areas where it could forage on new stands of aspen without exposing itself to its most dangerous predator, the wolf.

Reaching solid ground, I picked up the trail again and soon confronted another beaver pond, this one with a lodge half the size of a suburban rambler occupying the center. I took up a position on the bank and waited for the occupant to appear. The fertility of these ponds probably surpasses even that of the shallow bay where I started. With the flooded organic remains of the forest floor as fertilizer and the rays of sunlight penetrating the water, it becomes a garden of plankton, the minute plant and animal life upon which all other aquatic life and much terrestrial life depend. When I was there in early June, the pond water was profuse with tiny tadpoles. Also in abundance were dragonfly larvae, rambunctious hellions with heads resembling those of the adults, but fat bodies more than an inch long. They scooted through the pond by expelling water from their rear. Later, after they crawled up a rock and emerged as adults, some might be eaten by frogs. But now, the roles were reversed, and it was the nymph that very well might dine on newly hatched tadpoles.

My contemplation of pond life ended before the beaver showed; so I picked up the trail again, following it to higher ground, past outcrops of pink and white granite that sprouted 15 feet above the surrounding ground. The trail rose more quickly now, soon reaching a prominence from which I looked out over Kabetogama and Namakan to the hills at the far south and southwest end of the park.

My surroundings here were quite different from the beaver pond. Much of the trail traversed a rock ridge, some of it covered by lichens and mosses that had been baked by the sun and crackled underfoot. The exposed portions of the ridges were covered by scattered pines, but mostly by scrub oak, many of them no more than 20 feet high. The trail didn't show on the bare ridges. Instead, I found my way by rock cairns.

The Cruiser Lake Trail alternates between these environments—down along beaver ponds, sometimes crossing the dams themselves, and then up again into the uplands and across the sun-burnished ridges. By midday my legs were tired, my feet blistered and my back stuck by sweat to my shirt. The inland lakes, including Cruiser Lake itself, were oases of cool breeze. Cruiser is visited occasionally by fishermen; otherwise it is simply viewed by hikers who picnic and rest at water's edge. On this particular day, from all that I could tell, I was its sole spectator.

I pressed on, occasionally hearing a ruffed grouse drum and watching an eagle or osprey soar overhead. At one point I rounded a bend and nearly stumbled over a large black bear and a cub. I quietly retreated a few steps, gave the animals a few minutes to clear the trail, and then continued on my way.

By midafternoon I reached Rainy. A final loop of the trail follows the precipitous cliff—some 60 feet high—that plunges into the water. By the time I followed the trail down to the landing, my ride was there. We boarded the motorboat and sailed off into the big lake.

Water lilies thrive in the nutrient-rich still waters of beaver ponds.

ROCKS AND THE VEIL OF TIME

In the wake of retreating glaciers, 11,000 years ago, lie sculpted, polished outcrops of rock and "erratics" like this venerable one at Hoist Bay.

There's a place along the Cruiser Lake Trail where the wind has uprooted a large red pine. The circular, shallow-lying mat of roots brought with it several inches of topsoil, revealing bare rock. This rock, like all other bedrock in the park, is roughly half the age of the earth itself. The sight of a downed tree lifting up the entire accumulation of soil is quite common in this country, and whenever I see it I am amazed by how thin is the veneer of the present over the truly ancient.

Voyageurs National Park lies along the southern edge of the Canadian Shield, which stretches north and east to Hudson Bay in Canada. Though the rock here—visible in frequent cliffs and outcrops—is not the oldest in the world, it is the "craton," or stable core of the continent, largely unchanged from its origin in Precambrian times.

As I write this I fiddle with a chunk of greenstone, one of the basic rocks underlying the Shield, including part of Voyageurs National Park. This particular chunk feels substantial as I heft it— dense and green-gray with a hint of a greasy sheen. I am told that it was formed from lava billowing out of a crack in the earth's crust some 2.7 billion years ago. Its age really means nothing to me. There is no way I can imagine how old that is. Chronologically, this rock is out of context in my hand.

When this rock I now hold was formed, what would later become border country may have looked very much like the present-day Hawaiian or Philippine islands: active volcanoes rising from the surrounding sea. Oddly, like these tropical islands today, Precambrian Minnesota resided near the equator. The drift of continental plates brought it to its present position.

The emergent land was vulnerable to erosion, since no plants yet existed to protect the surface. Rain fell, gathering in rivulets, streams and rivers, cutting away the hard face of the land, returning sediments to the sea. This sand and mud settled into layers and after deep burial formed sedimentary rocks of various kinds. Severe geologic pressure caused the volcanic and sedimentary rocks to fold. Magma (molten rock still underground) intruded into these formations, cooling to form granite and changing the other rocks in the process.

Since these cataclysmic events, the rocks of the Shield have changed little, except to be worn down. While the rest of the

IN A GENERAL VIEW OF ROCK TYPES, *the geology of Voyageurs is quite simple. The far north-western corner of the park, including Dryweed and Big American islands, is underlain by greenstone. This volcanic rock held the minuscule gold deposits that fueled the short-lived gold rush of the 1890s. The far southern fringe of the park is the Vermilion Granitic Complex, or Vermilion Batholith, a body of granite 35 miles wide and 80 miles long, the result of magma that intruded into other rocks and cooled. Between the greenstone and granite, in a swath that includes most of the Kabetogama Peninsula, is a mixture of granite and biotite schist (a metamorphosed shale). In places the schist and granitic magma became mixed to form "migmatite"—sort of a chocolate-revel rock. Some stunning examples of migmatite can be seen at outcrops along the south shore of Kabetogama Lake from Chief Woodenfrog Campground, west approximately two miles towards Tom Cod Bay. Except for a few scattered formations that intruded into existing rocks about 2.1 billion years ago, the rocks of Voyageurs stem from major volcanic events about 2.7 billion years ago.*

continent was inundated by shallow seas or uplifted into mountains, the north country remained above the water and was constantly gnawed by erosion. As rivers leveled the land, the decay of plants built soil upon the rock. After two billion years, during which the bedrock may have been eroded to a depth of several miles, the surface had been sculpted by mature drainages. Except for the presence at various times of three-foot dragonflies or a huge *Tyrannosaurus rex*, the north country may have resembled Kansas.

This system of broad rivers and undulating plains, though long to develop, was not to last. About two million years ago began a series of ice ages that would affect the land far out of proportion to the time they persisted. The duration of the glaciers was a gnat's life in the history of this area, but they transformed the landscape into a pockmarked jumble of lakes and outcrops. At least four times the glaciers crept southward from the Arctic, each time completely covering the Shield, including the area now called Voyageurs. Since each ice sheet obliterated the effects of its predecessor, we in Voyageurs are left to study the results of the most recent glaciation, called the Wisconsin.

This last Ice Age began about 75,000 years ago with a global cooling of a few degrees in average annual temperature, perhaps caused by changes in the earth's orbit around the sun. In the arctic regions, snow fell faster than it melted. The land became covered by large snowfields, deep and heavy. They formed great bodies of ice—glaciers—that finally deformed under their own weight and flowed southward.

The forest that covered northern Minnesota—at one time probably similar to the conifer-hardwood forest today—evolved into a cold-weather spruce forest and then into tundra. Finally the ice sheet obliterated all plant life.

It is natural to think of these glaciers as global bulldozers, but such an analogy is misleading. Rather, in their movements and complexity of effects, glaciers more closely resemble rivers of ice and conveyor belts. As rivers, they were incredibly deep—nearly two miles at the center. Near their margins their surfaces were as rough and broken as any stretch of white water. As they flowed, they dragged with them boulders, soil and other glacial debris. The moving ice delivered its load to the end of the conveyor belt, where it dumped it in a pattern of hills, ridges and basins. When

Blue violets bloom for a few days, grounded in migmatite half the age of the earth.

persistent warm weather melted back the terminus of the glacier, the ice simply dropped its burden. Among the things carried and then left behind were large boulders called "erratics." One example is a huge white erratic on the south shore of Cranberry Bay in Rainy. The boulder appears much different from the rock around it and must have been uprooted from bedrock far to the north. Glaciers themselves acted as dams, trapping meltwater and forming huge glacial lakes such as Agassiz, which briefly covered Voyageurs and other parts of Minnesota as well as tens of thousands of square miles of Ontario, Manitoba and Saskatchewan. Sand and silt collected in the basin and were left behind when the water later drained away.

As influential as glacial deposition was, it happened mostly at the glaciers' margins, generally far to the south of Voyageurs. More important to the eventual appearance of the park were the forces of glacial erosion. When the base of the ice was at the melting point and ground over the land, it dragged rocks and hard mineral fragments across the face of the bedrock, leaving striations and grooves. Erosion occurred on a grander scale when water at the base of the ice seeped into cracks and froze, breaking the rock along existing fractures, so that the moving ice plucked out entire blocks of bedrock.

When the most recent ice sheet left Minnesota about 11,000 years ago, Voyageurs was a barren land of scarred rock. Much of the soil had been carried southward by the ice. Left behind were rocks polished and marked by glacial striations. The ice created "whalebacks," which have "upstream" sides that are abraded and gently sloped and downstream ends that are steep, where the ice plucked out a chunk of rock. Many lake basins in the park were quarried by glacial ice.

In the time since, the death and decay of plants and animals has helped to create a thin veneer of soil to which a dense forest clings for sustenance and support. But it is a facade, thin and temporal. Whenever a big pine blows down in a windstorm, we are reminded that the ancient core of the continent lies only inches below our feet.

A FOREST RETURNS

The boreal forest of northern Minnesota and Canada is a diverse collection of plants including bunchberry, or Canada dogwood, and groves of irrepressible aspen.

At first glance a large rock outcrop seems hard and clean, impenetrable, hostile to life. But get down on your knees, look at it closely and run your fingertips over its surface. You see, it is not smooth and sterile at all. The surface is covered with a multitude of lichens of different colors and textures. Each is a compound plant of fungus and alga that is able to cling to otherwise clean rock; the fungus protecting and giving structure to the lichen, the alga sustaining it, deriving sustenance from the slightest source of nutrients, moisture and light. Elsewhere on the rock look for thick dark green mosses that grow to a depth of several inches in depressions where water is trapped. Search out a crevice and find where a spot of soil has accumulated and now hosts a tuft of wiry grass. Finally, from a large crack in the outcrop grows a twisted jack pine that inexplicably has found root in what at first appeared to be lifeless rock.

It was by just such gradual encroachments that plants slowly reclaimed the barren land left by the glaciers.

Gradually, as the glaciers melted back, Voyageurs flouished with the kind of tundra now found in northern Canada— pioneering lichens and then mosses and shrubs. The decay of these plants provided soil in which new plants rooted. The accumulation of mosses, reeds and grasslike sedges in wetlands, where water prevented the complete decay of these plants, formed peat bogs. The soil was continually enriched so that as the climate warmed, spruce trees colonized the area from the south. Tundra dwarf birch became abundant, and tamarack and black ash flourished near lakes.

With continued warmth and dryness, red pine and jack pine, which had survived the glacial period in the Appalachians, spread quickly northwestward, replacing the spruce as the dominant trees. Paper birch and even elm became prevalent as well.

The climate continued to warm, reaching a peak about 7,000 years ago, when it was warmer than the climate today. Prairie extended far into central Minnesota, about 75 miles northeast of its present limit.

About 5,000 years ago the climate cooled again, favoring the red pine and jack pine again; birch, spruce and tamarack grew in greater numbers.

Such is the forest today. Voyageurs lies at the southern fringe

of what is called the boreal forest, a cold-weather community dominated by spruce and fir, but marked also by birch and aspen and in its southern areas by pine. The boreal forest stretches across northern Minnesota and Canada and from nothern Scandinavia across northern Russia, where it is called the taiga.

Scientists have learned much of the succession of plants by studying core samples of lake beds, where airborne pollen interbedded with mud, sand and other sediments. The muck from northern Minnesota lake beds shows not only pollen, but charcoal and ash as well. These are the residue of gigantic forest fires that periodically swept the north woods over thousands of years. The lake-bottom record displays a clear pattern: Fires became more prevalent as the climate warmed and declined when the weather cooled. Pines, aspen and birch flourished in the aftermath of these forest fires. The ancient mud has revealed that forest fire is a natural phenomenon and is necessary to the continuance of the natural forest. Fire is the gardener that tends the north woods.

The westernmost of the Wolf Pack Islands, like many other islands in Voyageurs, is covered by pines. The ground itself is profuse with low bushes and plants—most obviously in July, when succulent, tumescent blueberries adorn them—but overhead is nothing but the trunks and crowns of tall pines. To be in a stand of pines, whether red pines or the fuller white pines, makes me feel serene, as though I've entered a large, cavernous and empty cathedral.

In centuries past, fire helped create these vast pine stands. Even before people were in the country to set fires by design or accident, lightning would cascade into the tops of pines, igniting the trees or tinder-dry forest duff beneath. Under the most explosive conditions during a hot, dry summer, the blaze would race treetop to treetop, consuming trees and blackening hundreds of thousands of acres. French missionary Jean Pierre Aulneau wrote that as he journeyed from Lake Superior to Lake of the Woods he traveled "through fire and a thick, stifling smoke" and failed "even once catching a glimpse of the sun." Hudson's Bay Company trader John D. Cameron noted that "the whole Country almost from one extremity to the other was in a Continual blaze and stopt only by the snows of autumn."

In an 1899 report on Minnesota's pine region, H.B. Ayers of the

Fire recycles nutrients to the soil; it is the gardener that tends the north woods.

Translucent, waxy Indian pipe thrives along with sphagnum moss on the forest floor.

U.S. Geological Survey noted that "much of the so-called virgin forest has been burned and is now in the various stages of restocking. . . . Where undisturbed by cutting, the forest of today differs from that of a hundred years ago only as affected directly or indirectly by fire. . . . Thus it is seen that fires are not a novelty in these old woods, but have for hundreds of years been a prominent factor in their history."

The most exhaustive research into the role of forest fires in northern Minnesota was conducted by Miron Heinselman, whose bespectacled, round face belies the hard years spent in northern Minnesota. Heinselman drew elaborate maps showing the age and species of the forest. The effect is startling. Fire has created a mosaic of tree stands as complex as the most difficult jigsaw puzzle.

Heinselman concluded that even when few humans lived in the area, virtually every acre had been swept by forest fire—on the average of once a century. With particularly inflammable conditions, 10 percent of the forest or more could burn in a single year.

Many variables control fire. In a dry woods, fires can be spectacular, the flames feeding on the dried out forest duff and underbrush, rising quickly into the crowns of even the tallest trees and racing across the landscape. During a moist growing season, when the forest is verdant, the fires are more likely to burn small areas and die, or simply to creep along the ground, killing only the most vulnerable plants.

Heinselman's fire maps clearly show how forest fires have been guided and contained by topography—a fact well known to fire fighters. Fanned by a dry wind, a fire may sweep quickly up a hillside and through the uplands, jump a river and skip over a low, boggy area before stopping at a lakeshore. Consequently, today we find fire-vulnerable spruce, cedar and fir in low, wet areas.

Many other tree species have adapted to the continued presence of fire. Red and white pine, with their thick, tough bark, flourish in the wake of repeated minor ground fires that clear out the competing underbrush. Some giant pines display gnarled, gray scars, vaulted like cathedral arches, where over the years the tough bark knit a wound inflicted by fire. The serotinous cones of a jack pine spring open only after a fire, scattering seeds on a newly cleared seedbed. Sprouters, such as aspen, birch, red maple and

oak, succumb to fire, but their roots survive and sucker in the aftermath.

The last major forest fire in what is now the park began on the east end of the Kabetogama Peninsula in the stifling heat of July 1936, a year "so hot that people could hardly breathe," said one fire fighter. Until it was extinguished by four inches of rain three months later, the Kabetogama fire burned 18,000 acres. "It was a tremendous thing," said one man. "It looked like an atomic bomb exploded." In the ensuing 50 years, however, no large forest fire has touched this area. People, who naturally have wanted to protect homes and timberlands in the area, have made sure of that.

Without forest fires to sweep the undergrowth from stands of fire-resistant trees, the pine would gradually be replaced by balsam fir, spruce, cedar and birch. Within 200 to 300 years, the majestic stands of red and white pine would die of old age, and none would replace them. Blueberry, pincherry, aspen and jack pine, too, would eventually become scarce. The forest of spruce, fir, cedar and birch that would grow in the absence of fire would be susceptible to disease and blowdowns. In time, accumulation of downed timber would set the stage for a disastrous forest fire. Without fire, forest soils may lose fertility, as fire recycles nutrients to the soil.

The National Park Service is restoring fire to its natural role as one of the artists that paints the pattern of the forest we see today.

Brilliant mountain maples heighten the drama of a changing season.

BALANCE OF LIFE

The great gray owl is a year-round resident of the southern boreal forest.

The shadow of our little Cessna raced across the snow. Scattered jackpine stands added green to an otherwise stark landscape of blackened wood and white snow. Our plane slid downward, pulling into a tight spiral at about 200 feet. My stomach floated in my throat. "The population of moose in the burn area has quadrupled," James Peek shouted from the seat in front of me. "Wilderness ecosystems are dynamic." His words were oddly pedantic; I was more concerned about our rapid loss of altitude. But he was right. My face pressed against the side window, I looked downward at the promising signs of new life, even now on a wintry March day. Moose and deer tracks wove through aspen saplings that sprouted as thick as a three-day beard.

Peek, then an assistant wildlife professor at the University of Minnesota, was studying the recovery of forest, moose and deer in the wake of fire. He learned, among other things, that aspen, willow, birch and other moose browse increased 400 percent and that both moose and deer began feeding on this new forage only a month after the fire.

The animals of the north woods evolved over thousands of years in the presence of forest fire. So now, with few exceptions, birds and animals—not only deer and moose—respond to the profusion of new growth created by frequent fires. In biological terms, fire frees the nutrients locked up in a mature forest, making them available to animals. In more lyrical terms, it is fire that frees the jackpine seed that feeds the mouse that feeds the weasel and the great gray owl, whose bodies in death feed the earth that grows the jack pine.

Flora and fauna and the land are interrelated beyond our ability to describe or understand. The root of the equation is the sun and the nutrients of the soil, on which all the plants of the forest depend for sustenance. On these rely the plant-eaters—a varied lot that includes hundreds of species of insects as well as the red squirrel that feeds on pinecone seeds, the porcupine that feeds on pine bark, and the moose that feeds on saplings and aquatic plants. Beyond this are the carnivores that feed upon the herbivores—the broad-winged hawk that pounces on the mouse, the shrew that kills the vole, the fisher that ambushes the porcupine, the skunk that catches the grasshopper. In the

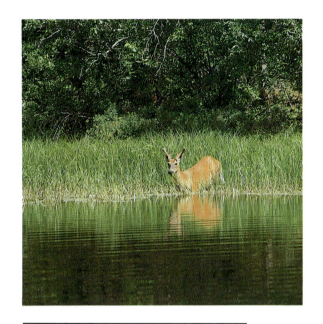

White-tailed deer are often seen feeding along shorelines in early morning and at dusk.

peatlands and other low, wet areas live the paradoxical meat-eating plants—the pitcher plant and sundew that capture and digest insects. Beyond this, of course, are the carrion-eaters and the agents of decay, the democratizers that convert the remains of all once-living things to nutrients that are returned to the soil. They are the turkey vultures, scavenging mammals, beetles and smaller organisms that complete this food chain.

Just as moose and deer respond to the abundance of food after a forest fire, other relationships in this web of interdependence may stand out quite clearly. The cycles of the snowshoe hare and the lynx are a case in point. Both are boreal creatures adapted to travel in snow with large furry feet that act as snowshoes. Moreover, the hare changes from brown to white with the coming of winter and consequently is called the varying hare. The bond between these creatures is strong indeed. The snowshoe hare is subject to multi-year cycles in its numbers—from abundance to scarcity—for reasons that still are not fully understood. What is clear, however, is that the lynx, which feeds so heavily upon the hare, becomes scarcer a season after the snowshoe's numbers drop. When hares once again do well, lynx do well a year later.

In some places the relationship between moose and wolf can be similarly close. Yet to the wolf's credit as a survivor, it is a versatile predator. So when moose are scarce, it can turn its attention to beavers or other prey or roam hundreds of miles, if necessary, to more bountiful hunting grounds.

In Voyageurs, unrestricted market, subsistence and sport hunting in the early 1900s eliminated elk and woodland caribou and decimated the moose herd. The decline of these large mammals has had ramifications that are still obvious today. Not only these large ruminants were affected; scavengers such as the raven and bald eagle have suffered from their absence.

It is conservatively estimated that up until the last century, the area now encompassed by the park contained nearly 500 moose, an equal number of caribou, about 250 deer and about 40 elk. These numbers changed as these animals migrated and populations surged and ebbed for natural reasons.

So the border country, including the Kabetogama Peninsula, was a rich hunting ground that fed the pioneers and loggers. During the gold rush of the 1890s, stores in Rainy Lake City at the western

LIFE SPRINGS FROM DEATH. *The sound of the bull moose crashing through the aspen and alders could be heard a long way off, though of course from the noise alone it was impossible to know what was going on. For that you had to be there. The pack of seven wolves, following closely behind, encircled the moose, harassed it, bit its haunches, flanks and nose, and finally dragged it down and disemboweled it. The wolves ate part of the moose and then left.*

The carcass of the moose lay at the edge of a small bog, near a small cluster of balsam fir. As the afternoon sky grew gray and dark, snow fell. A red fox followed the scent of the chase, found the kill near the shelter of the firs, and began to eat the flesh that the wolves had left. Later, two coyotes smelled the kill and chased off the fox. They, too, gorged on leftovers. Then, perhaps fearing the wolves' return, the coyotes left, too.

The next day was sunny and bitterly cold. A flock of ravens gathered in the trees above the kill. Several flapped to the ground and pecked meat away from the skull and vertebrae. They made odd croaking noises and were brilliantly black against the white snow.

That night a deer mouse, gnawing at the pelvis of the moose, was seized by a white ermine and killed. A great horned owl swept down from an aspen, clutched the ermine and ate it.

Several days later the wolves returned. The carcass was nearly clean of meat, but they cracked the large bones with their strong jaws and ate the marrow.

After several weeks the bones were covered by snow and were further gnawed by mice and voles that burrowed to them through the snow. By mid-spring only the largest bone fragments were left. They were covered by moss.

Soon they, too, vanished.

Moose, largest member of the deer family, are adept swimmers and are known to submerge entirely to feed on aquatic plants.

end of the peninsula sold moose for $5, caribou for $2 and deer for $1. Bag limits were unknown. Hunting—market and private—was extensive, even as these animals became nearly extinct.

The elk, whose presence depended on permanent herds to the west, were wiped out perhaps by 1910, certainly before 1920. The last caribou seen on Rainy Lake formed a herd of 20 to 30 that wandered south from Canada in 1924, according to one early resident, who shot nine of them. Moose, too, were nearly shot to the point of extirpation.

With the change in forest composition resulting from logging, white-tailed deer flourished as they fed on the abundance of browse and herbs that grew in logged-over areas. As the forest matured and the abundance of available food declined, the deer population fell. Without periodic fires, deer declined further.

The scarcity of large plant-eaters set off a chain reaction that affected not only wolves, but also many animals that fed off wolf kills, including bald eagles, red fox, fishers, bobcats and ravens. The wolverine, which occupied a precarious position at the very summit of the food chain, almost disappeared.

The impacts of the unrestrained hunting have reverberated through the food chain for more than a half-century. Happily, there are ways to repair the damage and reasons to believe the status of some species is improving.

First, the populations of two prominent mammals, bears and beaver, are healthy. They probably are as abundant as they've ever been.

Timber wolves, though they inhabit only a fraction of their original range, have stabilized in northern Minnesota and are extending their range. About two dozen wolves range in and out of the park. Their number probably will grow if deer and moose fare better.

The key to restoring the wildlife of Voyageurs rests with returning the large hooved animals—moose and caribou—to the woods in something resembling their original abundance. The key to this restoration may be good, plentiful browse. And, to bring this tale full circle, a way to produce browse is through forest fire.

AN ABUNDANCE OF WATER

One-third of Voyageurs National Park is water; expansive, deep water of the big lakes and shallow water in smaller lakes and beaver ponds.

To fly over Voyageurs in a small plane is to bring a map to life, showing the preponderance of water in this country. From a vantage point over the Kabetogama Peninsula, water stretches off in all directions. Rainy Lake and its hundreds of islands stretches some 20 miles into Canada. Across the southern and eastern horizons are Kabetogama, Namakan, Sand Point and (just outside the park) Crane. On the peninsula itself are two dozen small lakes and hundreds of beaver ponds. Equally educational is to hike through the interior of the park to see on a smaller scale the ubiquity of water—even on what a map purports to be dry land. Some low-lying hiking trails are routinely flooded by beavers that build some of the largest ponds and lodges that I have ever seen. In all, water covers 85,506 acres—39 percent of the park. Small wonder that the French-Canadian voyageurs of the 1700s and 1800s chose to travel by canoe rather than to slug it out overland like infantry. In this country, it soon becomes obvious that even on dry land, a lake or beaver dam is never far away.

The big lakes in the park—Rainy, Kabetogama, Namakan and Sand Point—constitute 96 percent of the surface water in the park. In most respects they are similar: expansive, wind-blown and relatively deep. Their bottom topography is rugged and unpredictable, as implied by innumerable islands and rocky shoreline, and specified by detailed navigational maps that show a thousand places and more to tear the prop off your boat. These lakes are linked. Boats (and fish) can pass freely from Kabetogama to Namakan (which some early explorers considered one lake) and Sand Point to Crane. Rainy takes in water from the others, though it is separated by the 12-foot drops at Kettle Falls and Squirrel Falls. Not surprisingly, all these lakes share the same fish species.

Nonetheless, there are differences in each lake's water chemistry and clarity, owing to variance in lake basins. In particular, Kabetogama is more productive because of its shallow nature evidenced by a profuse blue-green algae bloom each summer, which is lacking in the other basins.

The foundation of any aquatic system is the sea of phytoplankton and other aquatic plants, on which larger organisms feed. The plankton support an abundance of zooplankton and insects, such as dragonflies, damselflies, mayflies, midges, and hellgrammites (the three-inch larvae of the Dobsonfly; adult and

WHERE LAND AND WATER MEET. *The concept of an "edge" is important to ecology and the study of most individual species. Regardless of the habitat, the boundary between two different zones is the seam where life often flows. On land, the edge may be as abrupt as the border between a meadow (or forest-fire burn) and the forest, where deer roam to derive shelter from the one, food from the other. In a lake the edge may be more subtle—the long dropoff along an underwater point, where smallmouth bass pass from the stable haunts of deep water to shallow, rich feeding grounds.*

In Voyageurs, with its islands, bays, lakes, potholes, streams and beaver ponds, one of the most important edges is that between water and land. This is an elusive border that changes from wet weather to dry, from summer to winter, from times of an abundance of beavers and of beaver ponds to an abundance of predators.

Since glacial waters receded, these great lakes have ebbed and flowed with the seasons, erratically from year to year but with a long-time regularity that has shaped the evolution of the fish and other wildlife that lived near their shores. Depending on the vagaries of the season, the lakes would swell with snowmelt and rain, peak in late May and fall quickly through the summer and more slowly through the fall before bottoming out in winter, an average six feet lower than the spring peak.

With the low levels of summer and fall, waves washed silt from the gravelly reefs and points where walleyes spawned. Spring peaks flooded marshes where northern pike laid their eggs. Loons, too, nested in the reeds and rushes of shallow bays. Cormorants roosted and nested on rocky islands too weather-beaten to support vegetation or other wildlife. Beavers depended on a certain level of the winter ice to keep open the underwater passageways from their lodges to the lakes where they cached their winter food supply. Many animals had evolved to rely on the natural rhythms of water-level fluctuations.

Minnesota and Ontario Paper Company built a hydroelectric dam at the outlet of Rainy Lake and two ancillary dams at Kettle Falls and Squirrel Falls between 1905 and 1912, thus artificially controlling the levels of all four big lakes in the park. The

larva both look as though they may have escaped from the set of a horror film). Also important are other aquatic invertebrates, from tiny amphipods to the meaty crayfish. The latter is vital even to mammals such as the otter.

These invertebrates are eaten by small fish, including many species of shiners, daces, minnows, darters and the bottom-dwelling sculpin. These, in turn, are eaten by larger fish, including the game fish sought by thousands of anglers. This interdependence works both ways, as many of these critters forage on the remains of the very fish that ate their relatives. One night I walked to the shore to say goodnight to the water that had carried my canoe that day. By chance I shined my flashlight onto the remains of a smallmouth bass lying in shallow water. It was covered by crayfish large and small engaged in an orgy of groping, clambering, fighting and feeding.

Though the smallmouth bass plays an important part in these lakes, there is some question whether the smallmouth ever swam the waters of Voyageurs before settlement days. Unquestionably, lakes in the area were stocked by fishermen and from trains, railroad men dumping bass from pails and milk cans. Moreover, mention of bass generally is missing from the pages of early journals. Still, the ice age drainages in the area were sufficiently jumbled that it seems reasonable that the smallmouth crossed over from the Mississippi drainage, where bass do occur naturally.

The walleye undoubtedly is native to the area. It is another important predator in these lakes, feeding on yellow perch and other small fish, as well as invertebrates, such as the nymphs of large mayflies. Long and sleek, the walleye is distinguished by a milky white, translucent eye that enables it to see in murky, dark water but also causes the fish to shy from bright light. Saugers and yellow perch are close relatives that also occupy these basins.

Northern pike are aggressive predators that spawn in shallow, weedy bays in spring. Throughout the rest of the year, they hang in silty bays and elsewhere near weedbeds, ambushing smaller fish, especially yellow perch. They are the most common large game fish inhabiting these lakes, sometimes exceeding 20 pounds.

Other prominent fish are less well known simply because people rarely fish for them. Among these are the white sucker, whitefish and burbot (also known as eelpout, lawyer or freshwater cod, which it is).

International Joint Commission was established to set water levels on the newly formed reservoirs. Even now, however, no one is certain how the manipulation of water affects fish and wildlife. So research continues at Voyageurs into the relationship of fish and wildlife to the vital "edge," where land and water meet along hundreds of miles of shoreline and shallows.

The common loon, nesting in reeds and rushes, is an integral part of life on the "edge."

The largest fish of these waters is the lake sturgeon, whose name in Ojibway is *nah-ma*, from which Namakan is derived. Lake sturgeon attain their great size by scouring the bottom for clams, snails, aquatic insects and other invertebrates.

Lake whitefish, though they are known by commercial fishermen as "rough fish," are important food fish. They and their close relatives, ciscoes (or tullibees), are common throughout the big lakes.

There are more than 20 small lakes on Kabetogama Peninsula and on the stretch of land between Namakan and Crane. These lakes, ranging from 20 to 740 acres, contain native fish such as walleyes, yellow perch and northern pike. But some provide a fishery quite different from that of the large lakes. They contain exotics, such as largemouth bass and rainbow trout, that were planted prior to the park's establishment. The origin of other species—the muskellunge in Shoepack and Little Shoepack and lake trout in Cruiser, Mukooda and Little Trout—is uncertain. They may have found their own way here from surrounding border lakes where they surely swam.

The sustenance of aquatic ecosystems does not stop at water's edge but is carried to the land. The fat, glossy black bears that roam the park got that way by pouncing on the white suckers that wriggle into tiny creeks to spawn in spring. Great blue herons rely on stealth, long legs and stiletto bills to spear fish and frogs in shallow water. Kingfishers perch on limbs overhanging water and then dive down on their prey. Ospreys plummet to snatch fish from the water with their talons. Bald eagles do the same. Aquatic organisms feed the mergansers, cormorants, ducks and loons that dive deep into the lakes.

On the white sand of the bottom
Lay the monster, Mishe-Nahma,
Lay the sturgeon, King of Fishes....

"Take my bait," cried Hiawatha,
Down into the depths beneath him,
"Take my bait, O Sturgeon, Nahma!
Come up from below the water,
Let us see which is the
stronger...."

HARVEST FROM THE DEEP. *Border country has made fishermen of its people for thousands of years. Indians, as whites did later, fished for walleyes, whitefish and northern pike. Yet it was the sturgeon that seemed most important to the Indian fishery—not surprising considering their size, sweetness of flesh and caviar. According to one early resident, a 84-pounder caught in 1918 produced 90 pounds of roe.) As long ago as 200 years, the Ojibway speared sturgeon at Kettle Falls and from platforms at the mouth of the Namakan River. They fished for them in other ways, as recounted in the diary of one turn-of-the-century settler. In spring when the fish spawned in streams, the settler wrote:*

During the evening they would embark in their canoes and their torches ready for fighting when needed. The canoes were lashed together and the Indians set out.... An Indian would stand in the bow of each canoe with a long handled spear and a mallet made of birch root. The torch was lighted and the canoe passed slowly upriver, paddled by the faithful squaws in the stern. Then like a flash out of the night the spear was cast at the sturgeon which had been attracted by the torch light.... A short flurry insued [sic] and the great fish was quickly hauled to the edge of the canoe where its struggles were quickly ended at the resounding thwack of the mallet.

White settlers started their own commercial fishery. A typical operation was that of Harry Oveson, whose fish camp near Lost Bay in Rainy Lake was used until recent years and still stands. A sturdy, weathered dock juts into the lake. At water's edge is the ice house. The thick double walls were insulated with wood shavings and chips, and the floor pit was filled with sawdust. In Oveson's day, ice was cut from the lake in winter and hauled into the ice house, where it would keep for up to two years. Next to the ice house is the fish house, where the fish were filleted in preparation for packing into wood-plank boxes about 15 inches by 22 inches by 12 inches deep. Perched on an island on the inside channel of Rainy, the camp has a maritime aspect, especially in foggy or blustery weather, another reminder of Rainy's size.

On a typical midsummer's day, Oveson, short and wiry, saw the rising sun in his front window and pushed off from the dock before six o'clock. His boat was a 16-foot Alumacraft with two outboards—a 25 horsepower and a six as a backup. The bigger outboard jumped to life, sending up a plume of smoke as it burned the oil off the plugs, and Oveson motored out to his nets. In spring he would set gill nets with four-inch mesh for walleyes and pike, but during midsummer now, he stretched his whitefish nets—four of them totaling 1,000 feet, each nine feet deep with 5¼-inch mesh. Yard by yard he lifted the nets into the boat, emptying them of fish. He motored back to the fish house and put his catch on ice. He loaded the nets back onto the boat and headed out onto Rainy again, setting the nets by 10 A.M., before the wind rose. During the rest of the day he cleaned fish and packed them into fish boxes, each holding about 100 pounds. In warm weather he headed out again in the evening to lift his nets to keep fish from spoiling. On a very good day, he could catch, clean and pack 300 pounds of whitefish or 50 pounds of walleye.

During the heyday of commercial fishing early in the century, fishermen hauled their fish boxes to the landing near the Kettle Falls Hotel. "There would be about 200 to 300 people there to watch the fish boat come in, about two or three times a week," said Charlie Williams, who once owned the hotel. "When the fish boats used to come in, the fish buyers would stand right on the dock and buy fish— bid for the fish just like they would bid for cotton."

Though commercial fishing lingers, particularly on the Canadian side of Rainy and Namakan lakes, it is a dying industry. The work is hard, the hours long, the profit small. More to the point, however, both Minnesota and Ontario discourage the netting of walleyes and northern pike, which have become much too valuable to the tourism industry to be taken by commercial fishermen.

ANCIENT LIVES

I am accustomed to thinking of settlement as a wave quickly washing the continent from east to west. But the initial settlement of North America was something quite different. Crossing an isthmus of land and ice across the Bering Strait at some unknown time—what evidence we have suggests more than 35,000 years ago—Siberian hunters spread south and east. As the last Ice Age ended, they moved into the wake of the receding glaciers, as air fills a vacuum. Some of them must have stood on the edge of Glacial Lake Agassiz and looked northward over an expanse of water that seemed to have no far shore—that was as large as an inland sea.

These hunters used finely wrought chipped stone points on their spears, which they threw with the aid of atlatls, to kill what to us would seem fantastic creatures—woolly mammoths, musk ox and bison that would dwarf even our present-day buffalo. These nomads used fires and made temporary shelters as they pursued big game. Beyond that, we know little of them. We have found their artifacts on the prairies of northwestern Minnesota, but we can only guess that they also lived in the area we now call Voyageurs.

The big-game culture faded about 7,000 years ago, when people of the area began using stone axes, gouges and other ground and polished tools, and also knives, spear points and other tools of copper. The Indians of this culture, called the Eastern Archaic, scoured outcrops of Michigan's Upper Peninsula, Isle Royale and the upper St. Croix River valley for small nuggets of nearly pure copper, which could be hammered and annealed with no smelting or molding. The discovery of roasting pits for acorns and the seeds of wild fruits reveal the use of these foods, though large mammals, including the modern buffalo, also remained important. Also found at one Eastern Archaic site in northern Minnesota was the skeleton of a dog, the first evidence in this state of a domesticated animal. Only a few sites believed to be Eastern Archaic have been found in Voyageurs.

About 3,000 years ago the population of the area grew. People settled in more permanent villages as they made greater use of wild rice, a grass that grows in abundance along the shallow shores of northern Minnesota waters. These people continued to rely on moose and other large mammals, but also hunted or trapped porcupine, rabbits, muskrats, and beaver. Like their predecessors,

Early Indian hunters fashioned chipped projectile points.

they made their tools of stone and also used bone and antler for awls, handles and harpoons. Copper, shells, bear claws and bone were used for necklaces and other ornaments. But this, the Woodland Culture, was most distinguished by its striking burial mounds.

In some mounds the dead were buried sitting up, the legs flexed and the head resting on the knees. These bodies often were buried with tools, ornaments and other grave goods. More numerous, however, are "secondary burials." The corpses were set out on platforms, left elsewhere above ground, or were buried in shallow graves and later exhumed. Then the major bones were bundled and buried permanently, often without grave goods.

Just west of Voyageurs, at the confluence of the Big Fork and Rainy rivers is Grand Mound. More than 100 feet across and greater than 40 feet high, it is the largest remaining burial mound in the upper Midwest and serves as the archetype of the Laurel culture. These Indians probably still used spears, as well as harpoons with detachable heads to catch large fish, such as sturgeon. The Grand Mound itself probably was the burial site of Laurel leaders, because the effort required to move so much dirt would prohibit its use as a commoners' grave. The Laurel burials seemed exceedingly ritualistic. The brain was removed from the skull and the marrow from the long bones before these large bones were bundled together and buried.

The second Woodland Culture of the area were the Blackduck, who likely were descendants of the Laurel but who made greater use of wild rice, built smaller mounds with a different treatment of the remains and placement of grave goods, and made different styles of pottery. They also developed bows and arrows.

Hundreds of archeological sites have been found in Voyageurs National Park, most of them temporary campsites on the shores of the big lakes. These, in fact, are the same sites on islands and exposed points that modern campers seek for the same reasons the Indians sought them—a good landing, a ready supply of water, a sweeping view and few insects. From pottery and tools at these sites, park archeologists have been able to identify both Laurel and Blackduck sites.

What happened to the Blackduck Indians? This is impossible to say with certainty because they kept no lasting written records. But it is quite likely they were the Dakota, Cree or Assiniboin

Indians who lived in border country when the first whites arrived. But they would not remain long in historical times. They would be driven out by another revolutionary migration of people into a new country—this one originating from the east.

While our forefathers were living on the great salt water toward the rising sun, the great Megis (sea shell) showed itself above the surface of the great water, and the rays of the sun for a long period were reflected from its glossy back. It gave warmth and light to the An-ish-in-aub-ag (red man)." So begins the cosmic tradition of the Ojibway, as related by tribal historian William W. Warren in 1885.

> All at once it sank into the deep, and for a time our ancestors were not blessed with its light. It rose to the surface and appeared again on the great river which drains the waters of the Great Lakes, and again for a long time it gave life to our forefathers, and reflected back the rays of the sun. Again it disappeared from sight and it rose not till it appeared to the eyes of the An-ish-in-aub-ag on the shores of the first great lake. Again it sank from sight, and death daily visited the wigwams of our forefathers till it showed its back and reflected the rays of the sun once more at Bow-e-ting (Sault Ste. Marie). Here it remained for a long time, but once more, and for the last time, it disappeared, and the An-ish-in-aub-ag was left in darkness and misery till it floated and once more showed its bright back at Mo-ning-wun-a-kaun-ing [Madeline Island in Wisconsin's portion of Lake Superior] . . ., where it has ever since reflected back the rays of the sun, and blessed our ancestors with life, light, and wisdom. Its rays reach the remotest village of the widespread Ojibways.

Blueberries filled many an Ojibway birch-bark basket, along with raspberries, chokecherries, Juneberries and lowbush cranberries.

This oral tradition is the story of the Ojibway, the largest tribe of the Algonquian-speaking people of eastern Canada and northeastern United States. Their migration from the St. Lawrence westward through the Great Lakes region and along the north and south shore of Lake Superior was fitful and may have been caused by many things: disease, competition for land, war with other tribes. The result was the need for a spiritual revival and a pilgrimage westward until about 1400, when the Ojibway established their spiritual center at Madeline Island. Their migration brought them into continual conflict with the Dakota.

Already a woodland tribe, the Ojibway adapted naturally to the northern Minnesota forest. They brought with them the birch-bark canoe, a clan society, and an economy that was governed strongly by the rhythm of the seasons and the wild animals and plants of the region.

The Ojibways' spring began with the making of maple sugar. Often the Indians moved to a good maple forest—their "sugar bush"—where the sap was tapped, collected in birch-bark containers, boiled down to a thick syrup and further worked by hand or with a paddle until it took the form of granulated brown sugar. The first of the maple sugar, like other "first fruits," was offered at a feast to a *manitou* (an Ojibway spirit) along with petitions for safety, health and good fortune.

As the lakes thawed, the Ojibway moved to their fishing camps. They caught fish of many kinds in twine nets woven from twisted nettle fiber and also speared, set fish traps and angled with hooks made of bone. As snow melted and budding trees spread pastel green across the forest, families moved to their summer camps, where they opened the freshly thawed earth with hoes of wood or the shoulder blades of moose, and planted squash, pumpkins and other vegetables.

In midsummer the women and older children went out in berry parties, gathering wild fruits in birch-bark baskets. Blueberries, chokecherries and Juneberries were dried on frames of thin reeds. Raspberries were boiled down and dried. Lowbush cranberries were eaten fresh. Herbs, which formed the basis of innumerable medicines and charms, were gathered throughout the year, depending on their source.

In autumn began the most important season of all—the harvesting of the wild rice that grew at the margins of shallow bays, such as Black and Cranberry bays in Rainy Lake and Tom Cod and Daley bays in Kabetogama. As the days were cast in that hard-to-define light—perhaps a hint of yellow in the trees—that presages fall, the awns of this wild grass turned a rich purple, and the grain popped easily from the plant. One person stood in the stern of a canoe and pushed it through the thick beds of rice with a long pole. Another sat amidships. Wielding two sticks, each about two feet long, the beater with the first stroke brought the heads of the rice over the gunwale of the canoe and with the other stroke knocked the ripe kernels into the bottom of the boat. You could

To early Indians, autumn meant the harvest of wild rice, a cereal grass growing in shallow bays.

hear the sticks against the rice. *Swish, swish.* The sound of ricing was as rhythmic as the seasons themselves.

After the rice was dried, pounded, winnowed and stored in sewn bags, the Ojibway returned to their summer camp to harvest their gardens. They were preparing for a long, bitter winter. As the lakes froze, each family headed into its own winter camp, taking woven cedar or bulrush mats, cooking utensils, rice and dried berries. They built wigwams of birch bark layered over domed frames of ironwood or other pliable poles. From this camp, then, they spent the winter hunting moose, caribou, elk, deer and small game, such as beaver, muskrat, otters, rabbits and grouse. The brief days and long nights were spent hunting, butchering and preparing for the next day's hunt.

I have camped in the snow near a beaver pond not far from the shores of Rainy Lake. After only a night in the woods, I marvel that people, less well dressed and equipped than I, could endure an entire winter—a lifetime of winters. I can only imagine how they must have yearned for an end of darkness and cold, dried berries and the variable fortunes of the hunt, and looked forward to the season of maple sugar.

A red-brown moose, stick men, a canoe and odd symbols dance on a cliff on the Canadian side of Namakan Narrows. Dimmed by weather and time, many barely visible, they are ghosts of the Indians who paddled these waters in birch-bark canoes.

The matrix of these ghost images is dark rock marked by a vein of light feldspar, which, according to geologist Joseph Norwood in 1849, "must be highly esteemed by them [Ojibways], from the quantity of vermilion bestowed on it, and the number of animals depicted on the face of the rock." The paintings may have been a sign to the Indians who passed by that a *manitou* dwelled inside the rock.

Pictographs commonly were thought of as writing. But this pictograph, like the many dozens of others scattered across Shield country, says less of a people's (in this case, probably Ojibways') written communications than of their spiritual lives.

Their world infused with spirituality, the Ojibway concocted innumerable charms and medicines—substances to aid love, to attract worldly goods, to influence animals, to ensure success, to protect, to work evil, to undo evil. They fasted and meditated in

Pictographs, dimmed by weather and time, are ghosts of the Indians who once paddled these waters.

isolation to encourage the dreams that would bring them power and knowledge. Central to the spiritual life of the community were the *Midewiwin* or Grand Medicine Society—the men knowledgeable of spirits, herbs and ethics. Forever in the thoughts of these people were the various *manitou*, the spirits supplicated at every juncture to help in the hunt, heal the sick, bring good fortune. It was the *Mide manitou* that traveled the earth and taught medicine to the Indians. Subordinate to this supreme deity were the *manitou* at the north, south, east and west. Beneath these were lesser *manitou* that took the form of animals. Accordingly, it is hard to believe that the pictures drawn on the flat cliff faces, invariably perched above water, were simple communication. At the very least, it may have been a kind of spiritual graffiti—art depicting things or events laden with spiritual significance. Perhaps, even, these pictures were direct supplications to the *manitou*.

"To all appearances, the aboriginal artist was groping toward the expression of the magical aspect of his life, rather than taking pleasure in the world of form around him," writes Selwyn Dewdney, who tracked down pictographs across much of Canada and northern Minnesota. Despite his intense study of these puzzling pictures, Dewdney was never sure how literally they should be viewed as communication. Certainly he never found any surviving Indians who could interpret them. Nor was he sure how old they were. The artists who drew them probably mixed ochre with sturgeon or whitefish oil and rubbed the paste on the rocks with their fingers. As James Isham noted in his *Observations* of the 1740s, "the Glue the Natives saves out of the Sturgeon is Very strong and good, they use itt [sic] in mixing with their paint, which fixes the Colours so they never Rub out." Indeed, some pictographs described in explorers' journals nearly 200 years ago still are visible. Others depict guns and other European goods that became available to Indians in historic times. But many rock paintings offer no such clues; their ages and meanings remain a mystery.

"Standing Wind Woman" by Eastman Johnson, painted in 1857.

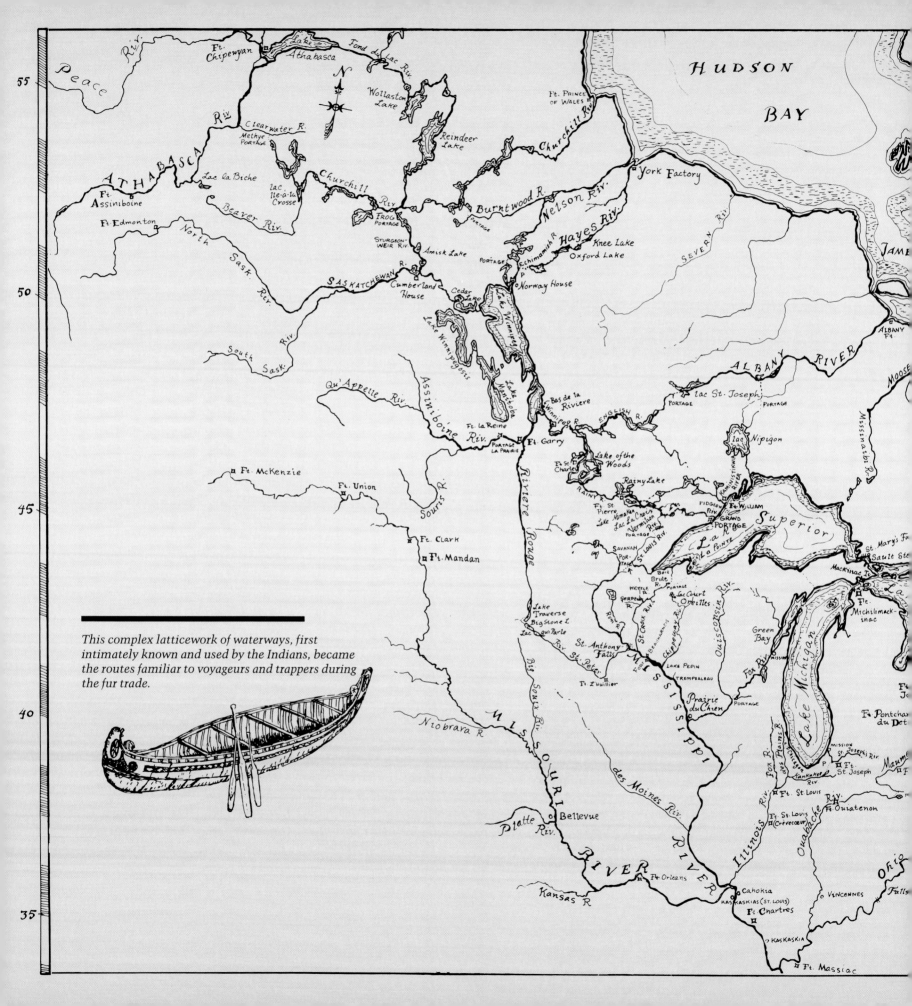

This complex latticework of waterways, first intimately known and used by the Indians, became the routes familiar to voyageurs and trappers during the fur trade.

55

Peace

Riv.

Ft. Chipewyan

Lake Athabasca

Fond du Lac Riv.

Fond du Lac Riv.

N

Wollaston Lake

HUDSON

BAY

Ft. Prince of Wales

Churchill Riv.

ATHABASCA

Clearwater R.

Methye Portage

Reindeer Lake

Churchill

Burntwood R.

Nelson Riv.

York Factory

Ft. Assiniboine

Lac la Biche

lac. Ile-à-la-Crosse

Riv.

Beaver Riv.

Frog Portage

PORTAGE

Hayes Riv.

Knee Lake

Oxford Lake

SEVERN Riv.

JAME

Ft. Edmonton

North Sask. Riv.

Sturgeon-Weir Riv.

Amisk Lake

PORTAGE

Echimamish R.

P

50

SASKATCHEWAN

R.

Cumberland House

Cedar Lake

Lake Winnipegosis

Lake Winnipeg

Norway House

South Sask. Riv.

Lake Manitoba

ALBANY

RIVER

ALBANY Ft.

Qu'Appelle Riv.

Assiniboine Riv.

Bas de la Riviere

lac St. Joseph

PORTAGE

PORTAGE

MOOSE

Missinaibi R.

Ft. la Reine

Winnipeg R.

ENGLISH R.

lac Nipigon

Ft. McKenzie

Portage La Prairie

Ft. Garry

Ft. St. Charles

Lake of the Woods

KAMINISTIKWIA RIVER

Ft. Union

Souris R.

Riviere Rouge

RAINY R.

Rainy Lake

Ft. St. Pierre

Lac Vermilion

PIDGEON Riv.

Ft. William

GRAND PORTAGE

Superior

45

Lake Nomakan

Lac La Croix

Vermilion Riv.

St. Louis Riv.

La LA POINTE

St. Mary's

Ft. Clark

SAVANAH PORTAGE

Bois

PORTAGE

Brule R.

Sault Ste

Ft. Mandan

KETTLE R.

SERPENT R.

Lac Court Oreilles

Ouisconsin Riv.

Mackinac I.

Ft. Michilimack-inac

La

St. Croix Riv.

Chippeway Riv.

Green Bay

Lake Michigan

Lake Traverse

Big Stone L.

Lac qui Parle

Rum R.

St. Anthony Falls

Bois des Sioux Riv.

Riv. St. Peter

Fox Plains R.

Lake Pepin

TREMPSALEAU

Fox Riv.

Ft. Pontchar du Det

40

Niobrara R.

MISSOURI

Ft. L'Huillier

Prairie du Chien

PORTAGE

MISSISSIPPI

MISSION St. Joseph's Riv.

Fox R.

Chicago

Kankakee Riv.

Ft. St. Joseph

Maum

Ft. Jo

des Moines Riv.

Illinois Riv.

Ft. St. Louis

Ouabache Riv.

Ft. Ouiatenon

Platte Riv.

Bellevue

Ft. St. Louis (Crèvecoeur)

35

Kansas R.

RIVER

RIVER

Ft. Orleans

Cahokia

Kaskaskias (St. Louis)

Ft. Chartres

Vincennes

Ohio

Falls

Kaskaskia

Ft. Massiac

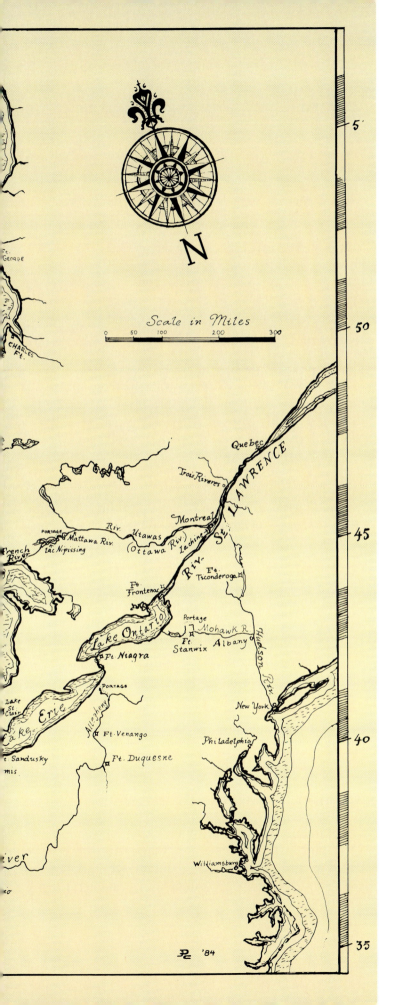

THE TRAIL OF WATER

Like many of us, Pierre Gaultier, Sieur de la Vérendrye, apparently suffered through his job to do what he really wanted to do. In La Vérendrye's case, his job was solidifying the French fur-trade route through Lake Superior and Rainy River country. His passion, however, was to find the Northwest Passage to the Pacific. So it is easy to imagine La Vérendrye's distraction during the winter of 1727–28 as the cold winds skated across Lake Nipigon, near the northern apex of Lake Superior, and whistled through the chinking of his fur-trade post. Consumed as he was, La Vérendrye sought any clue that would move him westward over the web of lakes and rivers that surrounded the Lake Superior region. In his investigation, he questioned a local Indian, Auchagah, who told the Frenchman of a route that led to water that one could not drink and that moved back and forth. Convinced that the Indian meant the tides of the Pacific, La Vérendrye urged him to draw a map on birch bark. The result, though it bore only crude resemblance to an aerial view of the country, laid out lake by lake and portage by portage three routes that began at Lake Superior, converged near what is now Voyageurs National Park and led westward down the Rainy River to Lake of the Woods.

Though the map never led La Vérendrye as far as the Pacific coast (the distances involved were far greater than La Vérendrye realized), it demonstrated that the Indians who lived in the north woods used and intimately knew the latticework of waterways long before their "discovery" by Europeans. Over thousands of years they had developed efficient routes from the Great Lakes far north to Hudson Bay, west to the Rockies and Northwest territories, and south down the Mississippi Valley.

It fell to La Vérendrye to establish a permanent French presence in the new territory. With Auchagah's map in hand, La Vérendrye in 1731 paddled westward along Lake Superior's northern shore until he and his crew arrived at Grand Portage, the "great carrying place" around the falls and rapids of the lower Pigeon River (now the site of Grand Portage National Monument). Frustrated in his trek inland by a mutiny of his crew members, La Vérendrye regrouped to the north. Meanwhile, he sent his nephew, Christophe Dufrost de la Jemeraye, to build Fort St. Pierre on the north shore of the falls at the outlet of Rainy Lake, about two miles east of the present site of Fort Frances. (Auchagah's map, in fact, named Rainy Lake *Tecamamiouen*, a Monsoni Indian word that described the mist rising from Koochiching Falls at the outlet.) The site proved strategic and durable. Since the erection of St. Pierre, many posts have occupied the general area near the outlet of Rainy Lake.

Just as La Vérendrye's travels were subsidized by proceeds of his trading, the fur trade propelled much of the exploration of the north. The mainstay of this trade was the beaver pelt. Old World hatters bought American beaver as a poor substitute for the increasingly scarce European beaver. The fine, downy underfur was separated from the stiff guard hair and then pounded, mashed, stiffened and rolled into felt hats. The fine fibers bristled with microscopic barbs that made the felt cohere.

Though the Europeans did not introduce trade to North America—Indians of many tribes had exchanged goods across the breadth of the continent for centuries—the presence of this foreign, eminently powerful people certainly put a different face on commerce. Goods such as iron axes were of a quality and quantity never before seen. The introduction of liquor and firearms had profound and often devastating effects. Ultimately, the fur trade moved not only Europeans across the north country, but Indians as well. La Vérendrye, for example, traded with Dakota enemies on contested ground and thus earned the Dakotas' enmity. As skirmishes persisted between Dakotas and whites, other tribes were drawn into the fray. The Ojibway, fearing for the security of the middleman position they occupied in the fur trade, allied themselves with the Cree and Assiniboin against the Dakotas. The Dakotas gained control of the Rainy Lake–Lake of the Woods area in the early 1700s, raiding areas as far east as Lake Superior. But with French guns, the Ojibway gained control of northeastern Minnesota during the mid-1700s.

Partly because of these hostilities, partly because of no compelling need to do otherwise, the Europeans for decades conducted the fur trade at arm's length. The British, who wrested control of the country from France in 1763, operated the Hudson's Bay Company from the shore of its namesake, relying on Indian trappers and traders to deliver furs to its doorstep on the coast. Eventually, however, independent traders sensed the vulnerability of such a link and smelled money as well. These competing *coureurs de bois*—"woods runners"—shortcut the system,

La Vérendrye as portrayed by artist Peter Spuzak.

meeting the Indians on their own ground and intercepting the flow of goods. In 1779 the competition organized in earnest as a partnership of Highland Scots known as the North West Company. Thus began the brief but colorful era of the French-Canadian voyageur.

Traders adopted many of the Indians' tools and clothes as they moved inland, becoming more and more like the Indians they dealt with. So it was that the voyageurs—some of whom served three-year tours in the wilds—looked and acted as much Indian as they did European, paddling birch-bark canoes, eating pemmican, using snowshoes and dressing colorfully in deerskin moccasins and leggings, short shirts of buckskin or wool, and tasseled wool caps and sashes. Many who served long terms in the north married Indian women and had children and in the process cemented relations with local tribes.

Unlike the independent *coureurs de bois*, the voyageurs were not freelancers, but paddled canoes in the employ of a fur-trade firm, initially, the North West Company. Coming from small farms along the St. Lawrence River near Montreal, the voyageurs spoke French and were faithful, if not exemplary, Catholics. Groups of men set out every spring from Lachine and crossed the Great Lakes with a two-ton load of provisions, pipes, pots, axes, ammunition, beads and other trade goods bound for the interior. After reaching Grand Portage, they exchanged the load for furs and returned east. Their bark canoes, 35 feet long or more, were called *canots du maître*, or Montreal canoes. They were paddled by about a dozen men—an *avant* in the bow, the *gouvernail* in the stern and the rest *milieux*. Their diet was salt pork and dried peas or corn; so they were called *mangeurs de lard*—pork eaters.

A different breed of voyageur took these trade goods from Grand Portage to the interior and returned from the bush to Lake Superior with furs. These were the *hivernants*—the winterers. If the *mangeurs de lard* were the apprentices, the *hivernants* were the journeymen, paddling 25-foot *canots du nord* (north canoes) over the rugged interior routes. Despite their size—under five feet, eight inches so they would not take much room in a canoe—the voyageurs carried two or three packs at a time—180 to 270 pounds. Legendary *hivernant* Stephen Bonga boasted that he once carried eight packs. Not surprisingly, a common ailment and occasional

One of the world's largest rodents, the beaver was the focus of the fur trade in the 1800s.

(overleaf) Voyageurs are depicted with historical accuracy and romance in this famous painting, "Canoe Proceeding along High Rocky Cliff," by Frances Ann Hopkins.

THE BARK CANOE. *Critical to the Indians' movements along northern waterways was the birch-bark canoe, a craft that at once was rugged enough for hard use yet light enough to portage, sophisticated in the graceful sweep of its lines yet simple enough to be patched or rebuilt on the spot. The bark canoe not only allowed efficient travel, but also fishing, ricing and hunting. In doing so, it provided a better life for the Indians who lived in the region.*

We may never know when bark canoes were first built, because boats, unlike stone axes and copper spear points, don't withstand decay. Any evidence we have is indirect.

Certainly by the time the first white explorers ascended the St. Lawrence River, the birch-bark canoe had spread the breadth of North America. The bark canoe rippled any waters flanked by the paper birch, from northwestern Canada to New England. The Europeans quickly realized the advantages of such a craft in exploring the New World. The Indians' canoes were quicker, nimbler, lighter and easier to build than the European rowboats. The canoe soon became such a pivotal tool in the exploration and trade of the eighteenth and nineteenth centuries that the fur trade has been called an empire held together by nothing stronger than birch bark.

The design of a canoe is a constant battle of a designer against the limitations imposed by materials. Thus, the American Indian was limited by the weight and strength of birch bark and the degree to which he could bend cedar ribs to form the narrowing hull toward the bow and stern. Still, the tribes of the northern United States and Canada produced canoes that were light, strong and fast in a variety of sizes and hull shapes that revealed a real sophistication of design.

The hull is secured from a straight, thick birch with no low limbs or major imperfections visible in the bark. The bark is sliced vertically and pops off the tree with the aid of a wooden spud. A small canoe can be built with a single piece of bark from a good tree, though typically several pieces are sewn together with the split root of the black spruce. Logs of northern white cedar are split out to form the wooden parts of the canoe.

killer was strangulated hernia.

The voyageurs' reputation for endurance did not end at water's edge. Once the canoes were loaded, they would pick up their paddles and put them quickly to the water, the paddle strokes beating the rhythm of their songs. They routinely paddled 15 to 18 hours a day. Occasionally two canoes would race side by side for hours. One such race had lasted 40 hours when the guides of each party finally ended the contest. Thomas McKenney, who traveled with the voyageurs in 1826, once asked his hard-paddling men if they wished to stop for dinner. "They answered they were fresh yet," he writes. "They had been almost constantly paddling since three o'clock this morning . . . 57,600 strokes of the paddle, and 'fresh yet!' No human beings, except the Canadian French, could stand this." From the morning to 9:30 P.M., when McKenney's voyageurs finally stowed their paddles, they had covered 79 miles.

Their ability to work hard and live freely determined their worth: "I could carry, paddle, walk and sing with any man I ever saw," recalled one man more than 70 years old. "I have been twenty-four years a canoeman, and forty-one in service; no portage was ever too long for me. Fifty songs could I sing. I have saved the lives of ten voyageurs, have had twelve wives and six running dogs. I spent all my money on pleasure. Were I young again, I should spend my life the same way over. There is no life so happy as a voyageur's life."

The area now occupied by Voyageurs National Park was the juncture of three important routes from Lake Superior, which except for Hudson Bay, was the most important entry point to the interior of North America during the fur trade.

The primary route inland began at Grand Portage and followed what is now the international boundary westward over more than two dozen portages into Crane Lake and then along the park's northern boundary. The voyageurs probably followed the border, making the portage at Kettle Falls (though they may have opted to shorten their paddle by making a longer portage at Bear River on the Canadian shore of Namakan). Then onward through Rainy Lake the voyageurs paddled, perhaps stopping at any of a succession of forts near what is now the town of Fort Frances. From there they continued down the Rainy River to Lake of the Woods and then along one of several routes that led to inland trading areas.

The bark canoe is built rightside up, beginning with the bark, which is laid out on the ground. Stakes are set around the perimeter to hold the bark up in the shape of the canoe. (Actually, at this point, it looks more like a hog trough.) The cedar gunwales are lashed in place, and the thwarts positioned and fastened to the gunwales. The bark is then lashed to the gunwales, and the canoe can be lifted from its building bed and overturned for final sewing with the split spruce root. At the same time, the stem pieces are set in the bow and stern to give shape to the ends. The canoe is again set on the ground aright. Split-cedar splints—each about ⅛ inch thick, several inches wide and about a yard long— are laid lengthwise into the hull to form a layer of sheathing over the bark. The cedar ribs, bent into a U-shape beforehand, are tapped into place, those at the ends first. As each rib is emplaced, the sheathing and bark are stretched tighter until finally, when the last rib is tapped into position beneath the center thwart, the canoe is ready to be sealed and set afloat.

Traditionally, the seam sealant was spruce gum melted and "tempered" with animal fat and powdered charcoal. Left in the woods with nothing more than a knife and axe, and given enough time, an Ojibway could build a perfectly sound canoe and paddle home.

A more northern route, adopted by the British, ascended the Kaministiquia River and followed an arcing chain of waterways that joined the customary route just east of Voyageurs.

The third and more southerly route led from Lake Superior up the St. Louis River, overland to the Pike River, north to the Vermilion and into Crane Lake at the site of René Bourassa's trading post, built in 1736. This route met the main route in Sand Point Lake, at the far southeastern end of Voyageurs.

That the voyageurs' customary route follows the international border is no accident. The treaty of 1783 between the U.S. and Great Britain set the boundary at "the usual water communication" through the area. But determining the "usual" or "customary" route was more difficult than the task would seem.

Finally, after years of study and debate, the Webster-Ashburton Treaty of 1842 fixed the "the usual water communication" along the Pigeon River, though the details of the border, which include 56 miles along the northern edge of Voyageurs, were not settled until 1925.

Fur trade was important to the land that is now Voyageurs because it provoked and funded exploration by the French and, later, the British. But changes in the fur trade itself ended the days of the *chansons* and *canots du nord*. By the mid-1800s wool, silk and other materials replaced beaver felt in hat making, and the price of beaver pelts plummeted. So it was that only a half-century after they had appeared on the great waterways of the north, the colorful voyageurs vanished into the past, as if enveloped by the early-morning mists of Rainy Lake.

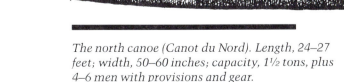

The north canoe (Canot du Nord). Length, 24–27 feet; width, 50–60 inches; capacity, 1½ tons, plus 4–6 men with provisions and gear.

A TIDE OF SETTLERS

Outcrops of migmatite displaying bands of mica schist signalled gold to early prospectors. The unproductive Bushyhead Gold Mine (opposite) on Rainy Lake was active during the brief gold rush of the late 1890s.

For decades, the Rainy River region could be reached only by water. But a fruitless and short-lived gold rush of 1865 led to the construction of a road to Lake Vermilion, which provided a route—though a difficult and complicated one—to the Rainy River area 60 miles to the north.

Partly to counter the territorial ambitions of U.S. settlers (including Minnesotans), and more immediately to quell the Red River rebellion of Louis Riel, the Canadians built the Dawson Trail from Thunder Bay to Winnipeg. Completed in 1871, the route traversed 500 miles and required 17 changes between steamboats, carts, canoes, stagecoaches and York boats. With the opening of the trail, steamboats began to ply the Rainy River and Rainy and Namakan lakes during the 1870s.

Alexander Baker, a Scottish prospector, squatted on the present site of International Falls in the early 1870s, becoming its first resident. An agreement with the Indians in 1873 allowed homesteading on the Canadian side of Rainy, and farms began to dot the valley. Still, the land now encompassed by Voyageurs National Park remained the province of the Ojibway. White settlement passed it by—until a man named George W. Davis camped one July night in 1893 on Little American Island, a mile north of where the Rainy Lake Visitor Center now stands.

Davis, a prospector, awoke that morning and began pecking away at a six-foot-wide vein of quartz that lay embedded in the dark greenstone outcrop of the island. He found gold.

People poured into the area over the Duluth and Iron Range Railroad, which ended at the iron-mining town of Tower on Lake Vermilion. Passengers suffered the 26-mile stagecoach ride over corduroy, rocks and mud to Crane Lake, where they boarded a steamer to Kettle Falls. There they transferred to another steamboat, which unloaded them—two days after their departure from Tower—at Rainy Lake City (across the channel from the Rainy Lake Visitor Center).

In less than a year, Rainy Lake City grew to a town of 500 with "three general stores, a hardware store, 3 hotels, a barber shop, two restaurants, a post office, customs office and 5 saloons," according to the town's paper, the *Rainy Lake Journal*. It was perhaps

Remnants of logging days when lumbermen floated logs to the railroad trestle at Hoist Bay for shipment to the mill.

GATORS AND WANIGANS. *Because loggers often used water to move logs, they devised various boats for their trade. Among the most distinctive used in Voyageurs were wanigans and gators.*

Wanigans were covered scows, some used to bunk lumberjacks driving logs down a river or lake. Another kind of wanigan was a floating cook shack. Half its 60-foot length consisted of the kitchen with its woodstove and storage area for food. Ice in the hold preserved fresh meat. The other half of the wanigan held wood or coal for heating and cooking,

surprising that any businesses could survive at all, considering the neglect they received. According to a visiting newspaper correspondent: "[I] went to get shaved. There was no barber in town. All were out prospecting. Then I wished to see the postmaster. I asked for him; he was prospecting. So I returned to my hotel, the Lake Shore House. The proprietor had gone prospecting. So it went, from the genial banker, Mr. Butler, and the editor of the *Rainy Lake Journal,* down to the mechanic and day laborer."

Mines were sunk on Dryweed Island, Bushyhead Island (where a shaft is still visible at water level on the south shore) and elsewhere. Ore was hauled by scow to a stamp mill at Rainy Lake City, where the quartz was crushed to free the gold. The Little American deposit became the largest and most productive underground mine of any, with a shaft nearly 200 feet deep.

Even so, the Little American was a hand-to-mouth affair. Within a year, it was played out, having produced scarcely $5,000 worth of gold. None of the other mines rivaled even that scanty production.

By 1897, only three years after it was begun, Rainy Lake City was nearly a ghost town, many of its residents having gone to Koochiching, which soon after was renamed International Falls.

During the late 1800s lumberjacks cut northward through the great white and red pines of the St. Croix and Mississippi watersheds, arriving in Rainy River country in the last quarter of the century.

Logging of the Kabetogama Peninsula and what is now the southeast end of the park did not begin in earnest until about 1909, when it was undertaken with great efficiency primarily by two companies. The International Lumber Company cut the very west end of the park and towed logs down Rainy Lake and Rainy River to its mill at International Falls. The Virginia & Rainy Lake Company cut much of the rest of the park. The next 20 years were the heyday of lumberjacks and the end of the virgin pineries. More than 40 logging camps would dot the landscape now enclosed by park boundaries. Said one old-timer who saw the final years of the operation: "If you couldn't log you might as well stay out of the country."

Until this time, rivers carried the logs to the sawmill. But the

and fuel (gasoline or wood) for the gator boats.

Gators were some of the oddest creatures in the loggers' menagerie. The name was derived from "alligator," owing to this boat's amphibious ability to winch itself across land where no water route existed. Introduced about 1910 and used up to about 1940, gators ran on steam or gas and were propelled by twin props. A gator was built on a thick wood-plank hull about 35 feet long. Mounted topside was a large drum, a powerful winch with more than a mile of one-inch-thick steel cable, at the end of which was a monstrous fluked anchor that weighed nearly a half ton.

The gator would chug far ahead of the log boom, drop anchor and release cable as it motored back to the logs. Then it fastened onto the boom and winched itself and the logs up to the anchor point. By alternately anchoring and winching, the rather small gators could move enormous loads, up to a million board feet of timber, according to some sources. Gators working for the International Lumber Company could haul a boom of logs from Kettle Falls 30 miles west to the sawmill at International Falls in five or six days.

At Kettle Falls, loggers would break up the boom and sluice the logs through the 12-foot drop of the dam. The gators, meanwhile, would "portage" on the Canadian side; the crew stretched the gator's cable across the portage and winched the boat over dry land on log rollers. But at least once, according to logger Fred Hilden, a boat took an unexpected shortcut.

An old boatman named Jim McCaw—who should have known better—attempted to lower logs through Kettle Falls with the gator boat. He should have anchored the gator and lowered the boom with the winch. Instead, he fastened onto the boom and tried to back the gator toward the dam, holding the boat against the current with the propellers. "The result was not only losing the sluice boom, but the boat called Archie *went over the dam, and it stripped everything down to the deck. You know there's the head works up there, and it just took the cab off and two or three men with it." The men were saved and the boat, which sunk in 80 feet of water, was snared by the cable of another gator and hauled to shore.*

Virginia & Rainy Lake Company ran railroad tracks right into the timberlands—more than 2,000 miles of track throughout northern Minnesota. "Steel crews" of two dozen men or more would lay tracks that were so makeshift compared to regular rails that one worker described them as "two streaks of rust on a wooden road bed." A trapper or "shacker" in the wilds along the border could now hear, not only the wind and howls of wolves on a dark, lonely winter afternoon, but also the sounds of logging locomotives in the woods on both sides of the border. One of the Virginia & Rainy Lake's main lines ran to the shore of Namakan Lake, where the company shipped logs from Hoist Bay.

For the lumberjacks, the work was dangerous; pay only fair. Living quarters were cramped and often infested with bedbugs. Loggers were killed by falling widowmakers (leaning trees), crushed by tipping sleds of logs, and injured in the perilous handling of floating or jammed logs.

Most logging took place in winter. Lumberjacks lived in wool: wool jackets, heavy pants, wool underwear. Nearly the only exceptions were their suspenders and rubber-bottom leather-upper boots. Loggers "skidded" the logs to rail or water with dray horses. Said one logger: "At that time a horse was worth more to the company than a man, it seemed. . . . If a horse died they had to pay for it. If a man died, they just put him in a box and shipped him out." If logs were cut near one of the big lakes, they were stored until ice-out in the spring, when they were dumped into the water, herded into "booms" and towed by steamer or "gator" boat to the mill or a nearby railhead, such as the one at Hoist Bay on Namakan Lake.

Still visible at Hoist Bay are immense log pilings that lurk at water level. Once they supported a railroad trestle over the lake. On the trestle was a "jammer," the derrick that lifted the logs from the water to waiting flatcars. Several loggers with long pike poles, hopping from log to log, rounded up the timber, feeding the logs to the "chainers," who waded in the water, throwing chains around the logs so they could be hoisted by the jammer. As each car was loaded, a slow but powerful "Lima" locomotive pulled the train forward to the next car. The fully loaded train was hauled westward up the Ash River (where the grade still is visible) and then south to the mill in Virginia, Minnesota, where 1,200 men ran the world's largest white-pine mill night and day.

View of International Falls from across the as yet undammed Rainy River. Circa 1900.

Early sportsman.

With such efficiency the Virginia & Rainy Lake operated in Voyageurs country until 1929, when the company quit northern Minnesota for the tall-timber country of the Pacific Northwest. But in those short years the huge, handsome stands of virgin red and white pine disappeared.

As early as 1898, with the glory days of northern Minnesota logging still ahead, Minneapolis sawmill operator Edward W. Backus foresaw the demand for pulpwood for newsprint and other paper. As that industry developed, Backus became one of the most powerful figures in the region and ignited one of Minnesota's most legendary conservation battles.

In an immense engineering and construction project from 1905 to 1910, Backus oversaw construction of the dam at International Falls to harness the power of what Sir Alexander Mackenzie a century earlier had called "one of the finest rivers in the N.W." The dam drowned Koochiching Falls and raised the level of Rainy Lake.

Soon, Backus had built ancillary dams at Kettle Falls and Squirrel Falls and was shipping paper from Fort Frances and International Falls mills. A decade later he was the fourth-largest paper producer in the United States. His holdings included development companies, sawmills, real estate and railroads.

Backus's plans required several additional power and storage dams along the border—from Lake of the Woods far to the west to Saganaga Lake many miles east. The dams, which were never built, would have covered several beautiful natural falls and raised the level of many lakes. Backus was opposed by cities and other parties that felt they would be damaged financially by rising water or that saw no benefit and did not want to share in the cost. Backus also became a target of early conservationists who felt rising waters would destroy the beauty of the area. One of the strongest opponents was Ernest C. Oberholtzer, who declared at a 1925 hearing on the issue: "When you destroy the beauty of that region, you destroy its utility."

Oberholtzer, a Harvard man and student of Ojibway culture, lived within sight of Backus on a neighboring island in Rainy Lake. He, too, had visions for the north country. But his plan was quite at odds with Backus's. Oberholtzer and his conservationist friends desired an international park on both sides of the border from Lake Superior to Rainy Lake and beyond. He promoted the plan

51

KETTLE FALLS HOTEL. *In 1913, a year after the dams were built at Kettle and Squirrel falls, Ed Rose recognized the strategic importance of the place, appreciated its commercial possibilities and built a hotel. A long, white, two-story clapboard building with a front and side porch, the Kettle Falls Hotel would become a favorite meeting place for travelers and strange bedfellows.*

In keeping with the bawdy reputation of the place, Bob and Lil Williams bought the Kettle Falls Hotel in 1918 for $1,000 and four barrels of whiskey. The hotel was built to put up loggers and the rising tide of other travelers shuttling between Crane Lake and International Falls. Within earshot of the falls people traded in goods of all kinds. A hundred people lived around the hotel in warm weather, loggers and prospectors among them. Ojibways brought in blueberries in summer, wild rice in fall, and furs in winter in trade for flour, guns, beads and sugar. Commercial fishermen hauled in 100-pound boxes of walleyes, whitefish and northern pike to be auctioned off to commercial buyers. And there was inevitable trade in illegal booze and illicit sex. Three "blind pigs" operated near the dock. "My dad used to have stills that a six-foot man could lay down inside of," said Charlie Williams, son of the early owner. He recalls that his dad moved him from room to room of the hotel as a half-dozen or

doggedly. His victories came piecemeal with the establishment of several areas, including Quetico Provincial Park, the Boundary Waters Canoe Area Wilderness and the rest of Superior National Forest and—the area near his home—Voyageurs National Park.

Despite these political dogfights, life in the country continued with a leisurely sameness. Boats of all kinds cruised up and down the lakes. The *Louisa Thompson*, a sidewheeler, became the first steamer to cross Rainy Lake to Kettle Falls. The *Ethel B.* ran mail to Kettle Falls and returned downlake with fish and once plunged over Kettle Falls on a bet. If you lived along the shore, you began to know the boats by name as they traversed the long fetch of blue and disappeared and reappeared behind islands and crooked shoreline: *Elizabeth B., Almar, BeeGee, Billy Magee, Koochiching,* the 50-foot freighter *Rambler,* the towboat *City of Virginia* and a couple of gators named for Indians, *Busticogan* and *Wake-Em-Up.* Large boats could be held up for days by log drives, and one, the *Monarch,* was sunk by a log.

Chief Woodenfrog and his band of Bois Forte Ojibway lived down at the west end of Kabetogama. To some extent they lived as they had for hundreds of years, drying whitefish, eating sturgeon, gathering wild rice in Black Bay, dancing, building bark canoes, wrapping their dead in blankets of birch bark and building small wooden spirit houses over the graves. Hundreds of berry pickers, many of them Indians, worked the woods from Orr to International Falls each summer.

International Falls grew quickly during the early 1900s, though as one early resident remembers it, "The streets were mud, the sidewalks were board, and everything looked very, very rough and wild." During Prohibition the woods were dotted with "blind pigs," crudely built shacks where liquor was sold.

The towns and woods were populated with various characters who earned local notoriety, an assemblage of loggers, moonshiners, prostitutes and deep-woods shackers who lived in an age when nicknames flourished: Poker Jack, High-Tit Tilly, Big Belle, Spittin' Jack Murphy, Cuckoo Anderson and Pigeon River Joe. The icy solitude of the Kabetogama Peninsula engendered stories—of people driven to the country by madness, of being made mad by it, and of dying under grotesque circumstances in it. "Catamaran" plied the lakes in his rowboat, his shaggy hair *more "girls" plied their trade. Since then, the feet of Charles Lindbergh, John D. Rockefeller and members of the United States Congress have scuffed the wooden steps leading to the front door.*

The National Park Service bought the Kettle Falls Hotel in 1975, though the place is operated by a private concessioner. The building was placed on the National Register of Historic Places in 1976. Two years later the Kettle Falls and Squirrel Falls dams, a nearby cabin built in 1910 and other historic sites were added to the National Register as the Kettle Falls Historic District.

The hotel underwent a massive renovation in 1986–87, the result of its original haphazard construction. The log foundation had rotted. Dirt and rocks from the hill behind the hotel had slid underneath. The building itself had sagged, stretched and leaned, complying with the changing contours of the landscape. At one point the door frames tilted perhaps 10 degrees off square and walls between rooms actually lifted from the floors. A remnant of this architectural decay is maintained in the bar floor, where there is preserved not only the bite of hobnails left by early-day loggers, but also an 18-inch rise in the floor that looks like a blue-ribbon sow hiding beneath a carpet.

flowing and water sloshing around his bare feet as he pulled efficiently at the oars. Said one long-time resident: "When he was rational, he was real interesting to talk to." Considered by some to be a drunk, by others a religious fanatic, by others simply crazy, he was found frozen, sitting on a piece of driftwood, according to one account. Another man, "Cuckoo" Johnson, was reputed to be a commercial fisherman and bootlegger and, as one story has it, met his end returning from a drunken foray in town to his home in the woods when he fell through the ice and died sitting up in a shallow slough.

During the Depression young men found employment in the Civilian Conservation Corps camps scattered throughout the country. In a program that was part make-work and part land improvement, they repaired the damage of logging and left a legacy of trails, log buildings and stonework on public land to be enjoyed a full two generations later.

The first sportsmen and tourists began showing up in the 1890s, though more arrived when roads were built in the 1920s and 1930s. Resorts of all kinds—from elaborate log structures with a country-club air to "ma-and-pa" cabins—sprang up on the shores of lakes. The people who fled big Midwestern cities for the woods and waters of Voyageurs country, most of them anglers, were simply continuing a long tradition of human use that began when Native American hunters first gazed across the icy expanses of Glacial Lake Agassiz.

THE PARK

As lumberjacks skidded logs through the snow on the Kabetogama Peninsula, as prospectors picked away at quartz veins in search of gold, the beginnings of a conservation ethic stirred the waters of border country. As early as 1891, the area was first proposed as a national park.

The voyageurs are gone now. The loggers and the Indians and the gold miners have moved from the park. What does exist here is a national park, created in 1975, nearly a century after it was first proposed. Its purpose, in the words of the law creating it, is "to preserve, for the inspiration and enjoyment of present and future generations, the outstanding scenery, geologic conditions, and waterway system which constituted a part of the historic route of the voyageurs, who contributed significantly to the opening of the northwestern United States." As much as possible, the land and water that make up Voyageurs are being returned to the conditions that existed in the days before people came to the country in significant numbers.

The creation of a national park has not kept people from using the area. Though hunting, trapping, logging and mining no longer are allowed in the park, visitors hike and ski the trails of the Kabetogama Peninsula, fish in the big lakes as well as the small interior lakes, camp on the dozens of sites scattered across the land and water, run their boats across the open acres of blue water and drive snowmobiles across the ice in winter. In doing these things, their tracks cross those of people who visited the land a century, a millennium, and ten millenniums in the past.

Signs of this long history of human activity are everywhere. Arrowheads and pieces of pottery lie on open points and islands. Iron rings, anchored in rock outcrops, remain from logging days when they were used in towing booms of logs. The beds of logging roads and railroads, though slowly growing over, still are discernible in places. And perhaps somewhere in the deep plunge-pool below Kettle Falls, as elsewhere along the voyageurs' highway, lies a set of nested kettles or a flintlock musket, once cargo of a *canot du nord* that capsized in the turbulent water.

Though the land has been well trodden, Voyageurs National Park is big enough and wild enough to get lost in. I have done it.

While exploring old logging roads north of Lost Bay, I strayed onto a trail that petered out between bog and jackpine forest.

Thinking it was the northernmost fork of the road, I backtracked to the junction and took the next branch. This soon emerged at a high cliff overlooking a jewel of a lake filled with beaver lodges. Unfortunately, my map indicated that another lake should have sat at right angles to the lake I was looking at. I felt a rising sense of impatience and an occasional twinge of panic. So I retraced my steps, back across outcrops and scrub-oak, down into the spruce, aspen and pine, across the beaver-flooded lowland and back to the trailhead on Lost Bay. By noon, then, I had walked six miles without really getting anywhere.

Once I got things straightened out, I could appreciate that a certain natural chaos still existed in a national park—unmarked paths, flooded trails, stretches of backcountry where no trails penetrate at all, country that can be reached only by bushwhacking. On the water, too, in the myriad islands and channels, it is possible to get turned around with no human sign to turn you right again. And that is perhaps the highest purpose of a national park—to give us enough space that we can know—for a few happy or anxious moments, hours or days—that we are in a land that is the way it was when human eyes first beheld it.

Voyageurs National Park is big enough and wild enough to get lost in.

Winter transforms a quiet pond edge into a dazzling display.

SUGGESTED READINGS

Densmore, Frances, *Chippewa Customs*, Minnesota Historical Society, 1979.

DuFresne, Jim, *Voyageurs National Park Water Routes, Foot Paths and Ski Trails*, The Mountaineers, 1986.

Nute, Grace Lee, *The Voyageur*, Minnesota Historical Society, 1955.

Ojakangas, Richard, and Charles Matsch, *Minnesota's Geology*, University of Minnesota Press, 1982.

Publication of this book was made possible with financial support from the Blandin Foundation, Grand Rapids, Minnesota and the Deluxe Check Printers Foundation, St. Paul, Minnesota.

The publisher has been given assistance and encouragement by Bill Gardiner, Mary Graves, Dick Frost, Joe Cayou, Ron Erickson and Lee Grim of the Voyageurs National Park staff and H. E. Wright, Lloyd Brandt, Carol Maass and Reed Christensen.

CREDITS

Design: Christina Watkins
Copy editing: Rose Houk
Production: Christina Watkins, Gladys Cole
Lithography: Lorraine Press, Inc., Salt Lake City, Utah

Photographs and other illustrations not credited to J. Arnold Bolz
  frontispiece: Glenbow Museum, Calgary, Alberta, Canada
  page 5: map, Pam Lungé
  page 33: Michael Budak
  page 36: National Park Service
  page 37: St. Louis County Historical Society, Duluth, Minnesota
  page 38 and 45: Wheeler Productions, St. Paul, Minnesota
  page 40: LaVerendrye Hospital, Fort Frances, Ontario, Canada
  page 42–43: National Archives, Ottawa, Ontario, Canada
  page 50: Koochiching County Historical Society, International Falls, Minnesota
  page 51: National Park Service

The recurring design is taken from a voyageur sash in the collection of the Minnesota Historical Society, St. Paul, Minnesota.

Quote on page 30 from *The Song of Hiawatha* by Henry Wadsworth Longfellow.

Copyright 1987 by Lake States Interpretive Association.

ISBN 0-915609-02-9